Examining Issues Through POLITICAL CARTOONS

Watergate

EXAMINING ISSUES THROUGH
POLITICAL CARTOONS

Watergate

Titles in the Examining Issues Through Political Cartoons series
include:

EXAMINING ISSUES THROUGH
POLITICAL CARTOONS

Watergate

Edited by William Dudley

Daniel Leone, *President*

Bonnie Szumski, *Publisher*

Scott Barbour, *Managing Editor*

GREENHAVEN PRESS
SAN DIEGO, CALIFORNIA

THOMSON
———✦———
™
GALE

Detroit • New York • San Diego • San Francisco
Boston • New Haven, Conn. • Waterville, Maine
London • Munich

Library of Congress Cataloging-in-Publication Data
Watergate/William Dudley, book editor.
   p. cm. — (Examining issues through political cartoons)
Includes bibliographical references and index.
   ISBN 0-7377-1108-6 (lib. bdg. : alk. paper)
ISBN 0-7377-1107-8 (pbk. : alk. paper)
   1. Watergate Affair, 1972–1974—Caricatures and cartoons.
2. United States—Politics and government—1969–1974—
Caricatures and cartoons. 3. Nixon, Richard M. (Richard
Milhous), 1913—Caricatures and cartoons. 4. American wit
and humor, Pictorial. I. Dudley, William, 1964–   II. Series.

E860 .W34   2002
973.924—dc21

2001055742

Cover photo: © 1974 Herblock

Copyright © 2002 by Greenhaven Press,
an imprint of The Gale Group
10911 Technology Place
San Diego, CA 92127
Printed in the U.S.A.

Contents

Foreword

olitical cartoons, also called editorial cartoons, are drawings that do what editorials do with words—express an opinion about a newsworthy event or person. They typically appear in the opinion pages of newspapers, sometimes in support of that day's written editorial, but more often making their own comment on the day's events. Political cartoons first gained widespread popularity in Great Britain and the United States in the 1800s when engravings and other drawings skewering political figures were fashionable in illustrated newspapers and comic magazines. By the beginning of the 1900s, editorial cartoons were an established feature of daily newspapers. Today, they can be found throughout the globe in newspapers, magazines, and online publications and the Internet.

Art Wood, both a cartoonist and a collector of cartoons, writes in his book *Great Cartoonists and Their Art:*

> Day in and day out the cartoonist mirrors history; he reduces complex facts into understandable and artistic terminology. He is a political commentator and at the same time an artist.

The distillation of ideas into images is what makes political cartoons a valuable resource for studying social and historical topics. Editorial cartoons have a point to express. Analyzing them involves determining both what the cartoon's point is and how it was made.

Sometimes, the point made by the cartoon may be one that the reader disagrees with, or considers offensive. Such cartoons expose readers to new ideas and thereby challenge them to analyze and question their own opinions and assumptions. In some extreme cases, cartoons provide vivid examples of the thoughts that lie behind heinous acts; for example, the cartoons created by the Nazis illustrate the anti-Semitism that led to the mass persecution of Jews.

Examining controversial ideas is but one way the study of political cartoons can enhance and develop critical thinking skills. Another aspect to cartoons is that they can use symbols to make their point quickly. For example, in a cartoon in *Euthanasia,* Chuck Asay depicts supporters of a legal "right to die" by assisted suicide as vultures. Vultures are birds that eat dead and dying animals and are often a symbol of repulsive and cowardly predators who take advantage of those who have met misfortune or are vulnerable. The reader can infer that Asay is expressing his opposition to physician-assisted suicide by suggesting that its supporters are just as loathsome as vultures. Asay thus makes his point through a quick symbolic association.

An important part of critical thinking is examining ideas and arguments in their historical context. Political cartoonists (reasonably) assume that the typical reader of a newspaper's editorial page already has a basic knowledge of current issues and newsworthy people. Understanding and appreciating political cartoons often requires such knowledge, as well as a familiarity with common icons and symbolic figures (such as Uncle Sam's representing the United States). The need for contextual information becomes especially apparent in historical cartoons. For example, although most people know who Adolf Hitler is, a lack of familiarity with other German political figures of the 1930s may create difficulty in fully understanding cartoons about Nazi Germany made in that era.

Providing such contextual information is one important way that Greenhaven's Examining Issues Through Political Cartoons series seeks to make this unique and revealing resource conveniently accessible to students. Each volume presents a representative and diverse collection of political cartoons focusing on a particular current or historical topic. An introductory essay provides a general overview of the subject matter. Each cartoon is then presented with accompanying information including facts about the cartoonist and information and commentary on the cartoon itself. Finally, each volume contains additional informational resources, including listings of books, articles, and websites; an index; and (for historical topics) a chronology of events. Taken together, the contents of each anthology constitute an amusing and informative resource for students of historical and social topics.

Introduction

*People have got to know whether or not their president is a crook.
Well, I am not a crook.*
                                   —Richard Nixon, November 17, 1973

On June 17, 1972, five men were arrested for breaking in to the offices of the Democratic National Committee, located in the Watergate apartment and office complex in Washington, D.C. Subsequent investigations ultimately linked the break-in to a series of illegal activities designed in part to secure President Richard Nixon's reelection in November 1972. Watergate became the name of perhaps the biggest political scandal in U.S. history. On August 9, 1974, a little less than twenty-six months after the original Watergate incident, Nixon became the first and only U.S. president to resign from office.

Nixon had won an overwhelming election victory in November 1972, and for a time many people in the United States agreed with his contention that the Watergate scandal was a minor affair that did not involve him. But in the time between the June 1972 arrest and Nixon's resignation, the American public gradually became aware of a dark underside to his presidency—a tale involving burglary, wiretapping, political "dirty tricks," secret bank accounts, undisclosed political contributions, perjury, and the use of government agencies to harm political opponents and thwart investigations. It was these mounting revelations that disgraced Nixon in the eyes of the public, led Congress to take seldom-used legal steps to force him from office, and ultimately resulted in the president's resignation.

Nixon's Early Political Career

Richard Milhous Nixon was born in a small frame home in Yorba Linda, California, in 1913. His parents struggled to make ends meet by farming and running a gas station and grocery store. A hard-working student, Nixon graduated from Whittier College, a Quaker institution, in 1934 and from Duke University School of Law in 1937. Following service as a naval officer in World War II, his political career began in 1946, when he ran for Congress against a popular Democratic incumbent.

Nixon's successful 1946 campaign began a remarkably swift political rise. He was elected to Congress in an upset victory that year and reelected in 1948. In 1950 he successfully ran for the U.S. Senate. Finally, in 1952, he was selected by Dwight D. Eisenhower to be his running mate in that year's presidential contest.

Nixon's early political campaigns established certain themes that would echo throughout his political career. In 1946 and again in 1950, he not only attacked the political liberalism of his opponents —Jerry Voorhis in 1946 and Helen Gahagan Douglas in 1950— but also attempted to link them with communism. (At that time, America was entering the cold war with the Soviet Union, and many Americans viewed communism as a serious threat to the United States. The possibility that Communist agents or sympathizers were working within the federal government was worrisome for many.) Nixon implied in his political speeches and campaign literature that Voorhis was a Communist, although there was no evidence to prove this charge. And he called Helen Douglas the "Pink Lady" (a softer shade of red, the color representing communism) and accused her of being naïve about the menace that communism created for America's national security. In California, voters received telephone calls in which Nixon volunteers would ask if they knew that Douglas was a Communist, then hang up. Nixon sought to exploit the issue of communism not only in his political campaigns but also in Congress. He gained early national prominence as the leading investigator of Alger Hiss, a former high State Department official who was accused of spying for the Soviet Union.

Nixon's meteoric political rise was almost derailed in 1952 after Nixon had been selected to be Dwight D. Eisenhower's running mate. Newspaper accounts revealed the existence of an $18,000 fund that had been raised on Nixon's behalf by California businessmen. Nixon defended himself in a nationwide address on television (then a relatively new medium). He denied any improper use of money, defended his lifestyle (his wife Pat wore not a mink coat but a "respectable Republican cloth coat"), and vowed to keep Checkers, a cocker spaniel he had received from a political supporter. Following the "Checkers speech," people nationwide sent in telegrams urging that he be kept on the ticket. In 1953, at the age of thirty-nine, Nixon became the second-youngest person in American history to become vice president.

By then, Nixon was a national—and divisive—political figure. To his opponents and critics, he was "Tricky Dick," a ruthless politician who would do anything to win, including distorting the record of his opponents, and whose financial dealings were questionable. To his supporters, though, Nixon was a hero, a youthful and hard-working public servant who protected ordinary Americans from the Communist menace and from an elitist and liberal political establishment.

Defeat and Comeback

Nixon served as vice president for two terms, visiting almost sixty countries on government trips and presiding over the nation's government when Eisenhower suffered serious illnesses. He was the clear choice for the Republican presidential nomination in 1960. However, he lost a close and hard-fought race to John F. Kennedy, losing the election by 114,000 votes out of nearly 69 million cast. Charges of fraud and corruption in several key states left some people, including Nixon himself, wondering whether fraud had accounted for Kennedy's margin of victory. Nixon's political career seemed finished after he lost another close election in 1962, this time for governor of California. He then moved to New York City and became a partner in a Wall Street law firm. He traveled extensively and continued to make speeches supporting Republican political candidates, including Barry Goldwater, the Republican challenger for president in 1964.

Goldwater's crushing electoral defeat to Lyndon B. Johnson left the Republican Party demoralized and divided between its conservative and moderate wings. Nixon emerged as the one person acceptable to both factions of the party. He presented himself as a

"New Nixon" who had grown beyond his previous ruthless political persona, and was nominated to run for president again in 1968. That election, like the one in 1960, was extremely close, but this time—by a margin of less than 1 percent of the popular vote—Nixon won over the Democratic candidate, Vice President Hubert H. Humphrey.

Nixon as President

The Nixon administration became noted for the president's heavy reliance on a close circle of staff and advisers, most of whom had worked on several Nixon political campaigns. Important Nixon confidantes in domestic affairs included John Mitchell, H.R. "Bob" Haldeman, and John Ehrlichman. Mitchell had been a law partner of Nixon's in New York in the 1960s and had helped run his 1968 campaign. Nixon named him attorney general in 1969. Haldeman, a former advertising executive, was Nixon's chief of staff. He became known for maintaining tight control over the president's schedule and agenda. Ehrlichman, an attorney, was Nixon's principal domestic policy adviser. In foreign policy, Nixon worked closely with Henry Kissinger, his national security adviser, to the exclusion of the State Department.

Nixon and his aides inherited in 1969 a nation at war in Vietnam and beset with domestic unrest at home, including race riots, widespread mistrust of the government, and a people still traumatized to some extent by the 1968 assassinations of Robert Kennedy and Martin Luther King Jr. They also faced several political obstacles. The closeness of Nixon's election in 1968 could hardly be interpreted as a mandate. Furthermore, Nixon faced a Congress in which both the Senate and House of Representatives were controlled by the opposition party—a political reality that limited his power to effect change, especially in domestic affairs. Nixon's efforts to shape government policy often clashed with the goals of Congress, and his presidency was marked by a tug of war between the two branches of government. For example, the Senate rejected Nixon's first two nominations for the Supreme Court. In addition, Nixon was criticized by Congress for attempting to "impound" federal funds Congress had appropriated for domestic programs that Nixon opposed. The Watergate scandal would later magnify the institutional clash between the legislative and executive branches of government.

Another factor in Nixon's presidency that grew in importance during Watergate was Nixon's attitude toward the media. Nixon had long had an adversarial relationship with journalists and media figures, believing that they were elitists who failed to give him credit or respect. Fred Emery, a British journalist and author of *Watergate*, writes,

> Nixon's relations with the press had been based largely on mutual disrespect. There were clear ideological problems. The bulk of reporters were opposed to Nixon's right-wing brand of often vindictive politics. Nixon let his contempt and self-pity show. . . . It was effectively a hate-hate relationship.

This state of affairs carried on when he was president.

Vietnam

Faced with a divided nation, an opposition Congress, and what he viewed as unsympathetic media coverage, Nixon had to deal with several important challenges as president. The issue that towered above all others during Nixon's first term was the Vietnam War. America's crusade to support South Vietnam in its war with Communist North Vietnam was costing thousands of American lives each year. "At the time Nixon came to the presidency," historian Michael A. Genovese writes, "the war was stalemated, with no victory in sight. It caused domestic strife, protest marches, civil disobedience, the emergence of a counterculture among the young, and a growing distrust of the government and the military. The war was tearing the nation apart." The Vietnam issue had effectively driven Nixon's predecessor, Johnson, from office. During Nixon's first term, enormous antiwar demonstrations were held in Washington, in some cases leaving the nation's capital seemingly in a state of siege. Nixon was determined to avoid Johnson's fate. His proposed solution was "Vietnamization," in which America would withdraw its troops, continue to supply the South Vietnam regime, and negotiate a settlement with North Vietnam that would preserve South Vietnam (and American "honor"). Nixon believed that antiwar sentiment and activism in the United States seriously weakened America's negotiating position.

In retrospect, many historians have argued that some of Nixon's actions concerning Vietnam prefigured and help to explain the

Watergate scandal. To avoid defeat while withdrawing U.S. troops, Nixon ordered several controversial military actions without the approval—and in some cases the knowledge—of Congress, including secretly bombing Cambodia, sending American and Vietnamese troops into Cambodia, mining North Vietnam's harbor, and bombing Hanoi, North Vietnam's capital. When some of these activities were leaked to the press, the Nixon administration resorted to wiretapping reporters and government officials in an attempt to find out who was leaking the information. Nixon also acted against antiwar protesters, believing their activities to be threats to America's security and international standing. Under Nixon, the Federal Bureau of Investigation (FBI), the Central Intelligence Agency (CIA), and U.S. Army personnel were used to spy on antiwar groups and protesters. In addition, Nixon's own White House staff sought to stop news leaks and harass and discredit Nixon opponents. In 1971, the "plumbers"—a clandestine private force operating from within the White House—hatched and implemented a plan to break in to a psychiatrist's office to gain the medical files of Daniel Ellsberg, an antiwar activist who had leaked secret government documents on the Vietnam War to newspapers. These activities—and the Nixon administration's efforts first to cover them up, then to justify them on the grounds of "national security"—came to light months later as the Watergate scandal unfolded.

Nixon's 1972 Triumph

Most of the activities of the "plumbers" remained secret during Nixon's first term, which culminated in the 1972 election that marked the crowning achievement of Nixon's political career. In sharp contrast to the close 1968 presidential race, Nixon thoroughly trounced his Democratic opponent, George S. McGovern, capturing the electoral votes of forty-nine out of fifty states. Nixon increased his popular vote total from 31.8 million in 1968 to 47.2 million in 1972; the margin of 18 million votes over McGovern was the largest of any U.S. presidential election.

Observers provided various reasons for Nixon's sweeping victory. Some pointed to his handling of the Vietnam War. Nixon's Vietnamization plan did succeed in reducing U.S. troops in Vietnam from 543,000 in 1969 to around 30,000 in late 1972. Nixon also ended the military draft, a step that took much of the steam out of the antiwar movement. By the time Kissinger suggested to the press on October 26, 1972, that a negotiated peace with North Vietnam was "at hand," the Vietnam War had been largely defused as a political issue.

Nixon could also claim credit for several other significant foreign policy achievements, especially concerning the Soviet Union and China. Demonstrating unexpected flexibility for someone with a long and doctrinaire record of anticommunism, Nixon sought to improve relations with both Communist powers. U.S. relations with the Soviet Union entered the era of détente (a French term for "lessening of tensions"). In May 1972 Nixon became the first president to visit the Soviet Union. The two cold war rivals reached historical accords regarding Germany, trade, and nuclear weapons. Even more memorably, Nixon visited China in February 1972, ending a long period in which the United States had treated the Communist nation as a diplomatic outcast. Nixon's visit helped pave the way for normal diplomatic relations between the two nations and is still regarded by many as the greatest single accomplishment of his presidency. It also greatly enhanced Nixon's standing among both world leaders and the American people.

Many observers believed that Nixon's success in 1972 was also the result of his attempts to cultivate the support of what he called America's "silent majority"—those middle-class, patriotic families who upheld traditional American values, believed in "law and order," and had had enough of the social turmoil of the 1960s. Nixon and his vice president and political spokesman Spiro T. Agnew developed this idea, lumping together as enemies unruly college students; antiwar protesters; civil rights and minority activists; elite figures in journalism, the arts, and Hollywood; and liberals in Congress. All factions were attacked not as "Communists" per se but as "radical liberals" who were weakening America, playing into the hands of its foreign enemies, and preventing the nation from realizing its true greatness. Many voters came to agree that McGovern, Nixon's opponent, was indeed too liberal or radical for them, and chose Nixon.

Regardless of which of the reasons were most important, political observers viewed the 1972 election as a great personal triumph for Nixon. No one could have predicted that a burglary involving Nixon election officials would lead to a scandal that would eventually drive him from office.

The Watergate Break-In

The incident that gave the Watergate scandal its name occurred on June 17, 1972. Five men were arrested at the Democratic National Committee offices in the Watergate apartment and office complex in Washington, D.C. The men were caught carrying lock picks, tear-gas guns, cameras, and electronic listening devices (or "bugs"). They also had new $100 bills and a notebook with "E. Hunt W.H." written in it. Three of the people, Bernard Barker, Virgilio Gonzalez, and Eugenio Martinez, were Cuban exiles from Miami; they were joined by Frank Sturgis, a Miami-based soldier of fortune. Why they would be interested in breaking in to Democratic Party offices was a mystery. The fifth person, however, former CIA agent James W. McCord, was soon identified as being on the payroll of the Committee to Reelect the President—Nixon's campaign organization.

The Committee to Reelect the President (CRP, or "CREEP" to its critics) was an independent political organization separate from the Republican Party. Created for the sole purpose of helping Nixon's reelection campaign, the CRP was ostensibly involved in such activities as preparing and circulating campaign literature, appealing for votes, and raising funds. At its head was John Mitchell, who had resigned as attorney general to take over the post. CRP's connection to the Watergate break-in was a potentially embarrassing development for the president.

Law enforcement officials traced the money found on the five men arrested at the Watergate complex to a CRP account. However, Mitchell issued a statement denying any CRP connection to the break-in; he resigned his post and returned to private law practice a few days later on July 1. Presidential press secretary Ron Ziegler described Watergate as a "third-rate burglary attempt" on June 19. At a July 22 press conference, Nixon himself stated that "the White House has had no involvement in this particular incident." A few weeks later, on August 29, he again assured the American people that White House counsel John Dean had conducted his own in-house investigation and had concluded that "no one in this administration, presently employed, was involved in this very bizarre incident." Author Barbara Silberdick Feinberg writes,

> After listening to these statements, few Americans had reason to doubt that the break-in was just an isolated event. Be-

sides, dirty politics in an election year was almost a national tradition. That is why the public tended to refer to the break-in as a caper and a prank, rather than a crime. People quickly lost interest in the failed bugging of Democratic Headquarters, and directed their attention elsewhere.

In September 1972, federal prosecutors succeeded in winning indictments from a federal grand jury against the five burglars and two others—White House consultant E. Howard Hunt (it was his name in the notebook found at the scene of the crime) and CRP counsel G. Gordon Liddy. The indictments did little to add to the scandal. Watergate remained an ongoing, but relatively minor, news story until after Nixon's election triumph in November 1972.

Collapse of a Cover-Up

In early 1973, the Watergate scandal seemed to be a bizarre and isolated incident. The seven indicted defendants either pleaded or were found guilty in a January trial. Federal prosecutors argued that Liddy had authorized the break-in without the knowledge and consent of his superiors. The presiding judge, John Sirica, suspected that higher Nixon officials were involved. He offered reduced sentences to the defendants if they provided more information.

Within a few months, the Liddy-as-rogue-mastermind story had collapsed, and Americans knew that an organized cover-up effort involving high White House officials had been hindering the investigation and prosecution of the case since the original June arrests. In March 1973, one of the Watergate defendants, McCord, came forward to Judge Sirica, claiming that administration officials, including CRP deputy chairman Jeb Magruder and White House counsel John Dean, had engaged in bribery and perjury. Soon, Magruder, Dean, and other CRP and White House officials began to cooperate with federal prosecutors. A special Senate committee to investigate campaign practices began televised hearings in May. Over the next several months, a rapt nation listened as administration officials answered questions about the Watergate break-in and subsequent cover-up.

As it became increasingly clear that high Nixon administration officials were somehow involved in the burgeoning Watergate scandal, many people wondered whether career federal prosecutors who were employed by the attorney general and the president could adequately investigate and prosecute the case. Many called for an outside special prosecutor not beholden to the president to be brought in to oversee the investigation. In April 1973, in the face of mounting revelations about Watergate, President Nixon appointed a new attorney general, Elliot Richardson, to replace the dismissed Richard Kleindienst. Both Richardson and Nixon agreed to the appointment of a special prosecutor for Watergate. In May 1973, Richardson (without consulting the president) named Harvard Law School professor Archibald Cox to the position. Cox took over the task of investigating the Watergate case and presenting evidence before the federal grand jury that had issued the September 1972 indictments and that was still hearing evidence about Watergate. "The Special Prosecutor's Office," writes historian Kim McQuaid, "was an odd bureaucratic creation. It was *in* the executive branch, but not *of* it."

By the middle of 1973, Watergate dominated American news. From Senate hearings, reports and leaks from the special prosecutor's office, and media investigations, Americans over the next year received the following information:

- John Mitchell had approved the planting of eavesdropping devices in the Watergate offices of the Democratic National Committee.

- Nixon administration officials, with the president's knowledge and approval, had hindered the work of the federal investigators in order to cover up any links between the Watergate burglars and the Nixon administration, including destroying or hiding incriminating evidence and paying large sums of money to the burglars for their silence.

- The CRP had secretly collected large amounts of money from corporations with promises of favors or threats of government retaliation.

- The August 1972 report by John Dean that supposedly had cleared officials of Watergate involvement did not exist.

- The "plumbers" unit had broken in to Ellsberg's psychiatrist's office.

- The Nixon administration had created and maintained an "enemies list" of Nixon's political opponents who were supposed to be targeted for harassment by the Internal Revenue Service and other government agencies.

- CRP personnel had engaged in various political "dirty tricks" against Edmund S. Muskie and other Democratic presidential candidates deemed stronger than McGovern, the eventual nominee; these tricks included espionage reports from Muskie's chauffeur, spreading false rumors about the sexual preference of candidates, and forging embarrassing letters in their names.

- Nixon had used federal funds to make improvements to his personal homes in Florida and California and had taken questionable deductions on his income taxes for donating his papers to the Library of Congress.

- Nixon had illegally ordered wiretaps (that is, without obtaining court approval) on the phones of newspaper reporters as early as 1969 in order to protect the secrecy of American bombing raids over Cambodia.

- Nixon had installed a tape system in 1971 that automatically recorded most of his conversations in the White House.

The disclosure of the existence of Nixon's secret tapes was a turning point. Most of the damaging allegations against Nixon came from witnesses, such as Dean, who were themselves involved in Watergate and were not fully credible. A question repeatedly posed by Senator Howard Baker, the ranking Republican on the Senate Watergate Committee, had been, "What did the president know, and when did he know it?" This seemed impossible to determine—until the revelation that conversations had been taped. Here seemed to be a golden opportunity to uncover the truth. The Senate committee quickly requested the tapes from Nixon. Nixon refused to turn them over, arguing that as president, he possessed the "executive privilege" to keep his private conversations confidential.

The tapes became subject to a tug of war not only between the president and Congress, but also between the president and the special prosecutor's office. Shortly after Congress was rebuffed in its attempts to get some of the president's tapes, Cox subpoenaed nine tapes. When Nixon refused to turn them over, Cox appealed to Judge Sirica, who ordered Nixon to comply. Nixon again refused, arguing that a president was immune from such judicial orders and that only the president could decide which communications could be disclosed. But a U.S. court of appeals upheld Sirica's order.

On October 20, 1973, Nixon tried to have Attorney General Richardson fire Cox, but Richardson instead resigned, as did his deputy. Nixon finally succeeded in naming Solicitor General Robert H. Bork as acting attorney general and in dismissing Cox. But these actions, which were subsequently referred to as the "Saturday Night Massacre," produced a storm of public criticism. Facing a public relations crisis, Nixon agreed to surrender the nine tapes to Sirica and to appoint Texas attorney Leon Jaworski to take Cox's place, giving Jaworski even more independence from presidential oversight than Cox had had. Nixon's credibility was further damaged in November when his lawyers told Sirica that two of the nine subpoenaed tapes did not exist and a third contained a mysterious eighteen-minute gap. Nixon refused to release any additional tapes or tape transcripts to the Senate or to the special prosecutor.

Impeachment and Indictments

In the wake of the Saturday Night Massacre, Congress began to discuss the possibility of impeaching Nixon. The Constitution gives power to Congress to impeach and remove the president or other government officials for "Treason, Bribery, or other high Crimes and Misdemeanors." This tool had been used against a president only once in American history (Andrew Johnson in 1868), but on October 30, 1973, members of the House of Representatives began to consider how impeachment could be done. A few months later, the House officially voted to have the House Judiciary Committee begin an impeachment investigation. The committee began holding closed hearings on May 9, with public (and televised) sessions in July. The House also joined the Senate and the special prosecutor's office in asking for additional tapes from Nixon as evidence.

While attention was focused on Watergate, America was rocked by a different political scandal that hit the nation's leadership. On October 10, 1973, Vice President Spiro T. Agnew suddenly resigned after pleading no contest to charges of income tax evasion. Under terms of the recently adopted Twenty-Fifth Amendment to the Constitution, Nixon appointed Gerald R. Ford, a respected veteran Republican congressman from Michigan, to be vice president. Ford was confirmed by Congress and took the oath of office on December 6, 1973.

Meanwhile, as Congress was debating impeachment, Jaworski was continuing his investigation. On March 1, 1974, he convinced the federal grand jury to issue criminal indictments against John Mitchell, H.R. Haldeman, John Ehrlichman, and four other former administration officials. In addition, the jury named Nixon as an "unindicted co-conspirator." In April, Jaworski issued Nixon yet another subpoena, this time for sixty-four tapes of conversations related to the Watergate cover-up. The issue ultimately reached the Supreme Court, which on July 24 ruled 8-0 that Nixon must release the tapes. One of the tapes Nixon was compelled to relinquish revealed that the president had actively conspired to hinder the Watergate investigation on June 23, 1972, six days after the original arrests. When it was released to the public on August 5, the so-called smoking gun tape stunned Nixon defenders in Congress and decimated Nixon's standing in public opinion.

Resignation and Pardon

The House Judiciary Committee approved three articles of impeachment against Nixon at the end of July. The articles, which drew bipartisan support, accused the president of obstruction of justice, abuse of power, and contempt of Congress. The next step in the impeachment process would have been a vote by the full House, followed by a trial conducted in the Senate. Facing almost certain impeachment by the House and likely conviction by the Senate, Nixon instead made the painful decision to step down. On August 8, he announced on national television that he would resign from the office of president of the United States, effective at noon the next day. "I deeply regret any injuries that may have been done in the course of the events that led to this decision," he stated in what would be the closest he ever would come to an admission of wrongdoing. "I would say only that if some of my judgments were wrong —and some were wrong—they were made in what I believed at the time to be the best interest of the nation."

One month later, the new president, Gerald Ford, issued a "full, free and absolute pardon" to Nixon, thus cutting off any further legal actions against the ex-president. Although Nixon himself escaped criminal conviction, more than thirty people, including high government officials, were charged and convicted of crimes. John Dean served four months in prison. Ehrlichman served eighteen months. Mitchell, who became the first former attorney general to spend time in a federal prison, was released in 1979 after serving nineteen months. He was the last Watergate defendant to be freed.

The Legacy of Watergate

Watergate left a lasting legacy on the public image and functioning of American government. It resulted in the suffix "gate" being attached to subsequent presidential and political scandals. Watergate temporarily damaged the political fortunes of the Republican Party and contributed to Gerald Ford's failure to win the 1976 presidential election. The scandal also is credited with bolstering the image of investigative reporting and encouraging journalists to aggressively probe and report on scandals in subsequent presidential administrations. Because of Watergate (and also, to some extent, the Vietnam War), the American public has become far more cynical regarding official government pronouncements and the honesty of politicians. According to polls, three-quarters of the American public in 1964 said they trusted their national government to do the right thing; by 1974 only 36 percent still trusted the government.

Whether or not the American constitutional system of government was ultimately vindicated by how the Watergate scandal turned out remains a source of disagreement. Historian Irwin Unger writes,

> Some Americans saw reasons for optimism in the outcome of Watergate. The "system had worked," they said; the villains had been caught and punished, and honest, constitutional government had been restored. Others were not so sure. Nixon had, after all, been reelected in a landslide and might easily have gotten away with it all if a very few lucky events had happened differently. Many Americans could not avoid feeling more cynical than ever about the honesty of politicians and more skeptical about the effectiveness of the nation's political system.

Finally, an important Watergate legacy was its indelible mark on Nixon's historical reputation. Nixon himself retired with a full presidential pension. He later attempted to rehabilitate his public career as an elder statesman, publishing books and articles on foreign policy and advising U.S. presidents. Despite some success in the last of his political comebacks, his leading legacy, most historians agreed at the time of his death in 1994, remained the Watergate scandal that forced him to resign.

Chapter 1

A Third-Rate Burglary

Preface

The story of Watergate began with the arrest of five burglars at Democratic Party offices in the Watergate hotel and office complex in Washington, D.C., in the early morning hours of June 17, 1972. The five people arrested possessed electronic listening devices, or "bugs," as well as cameras, rubber gloves, and large amounts of cash. At the time of their arrest, they were repairing previously installed bugs from an earlier break-in. One of them, James McCord, a former Central Intellgence Agency (CIA) agent, was employed by the Committee to Reelect the President (CRP), President Richard Nixon's campaign organization. Later G. Gordon Liddy, counsel to CRP, and E. Howard Hunt, a White House consultant, were arrested in connection with the break-in.

At first, the Watergate break-in seemed like a minor, if mysterious, story. The *New York Times* ran a short article about the arrests on page thirty of its June 18 edition; its coverage was typical among national newspapers. Presidential spokesperson Ron Ziegler dismissed the event as a "third-rate burglary attempt." President Nixon himself declared on June 22 that no one in the White House was involved in the burglary and that "attempted surveillance" had no place in the governmental process.

Over the next several months some newspaper reporters continued to investigate the break-in. Two *Washington Post* reporters, Bob Woodward and Carl Bernstein, published a series of stories probing a mysterious tangle of political espionage against Democratic presidential candidates and connected them to officials at the Nixon White House and CRP. But Watergate remained a confusing story to most Americans. George S. McGovern, a senator who was Nixon's opponent in the 1972 presidential election, attempted to raise Watergate as an issue but was unable to close the gap between himself and the president in the polls. Other issues, such as negotiations to end the Vietnam War, loomed larger.

A federal grand jury indicted the seven defendants for burglary, conspiracy, and illegal wiretapping on September 15, 1972. Department of Justice officials issued a statement that they had "absolutely no evidence that others should be charged." The defendants all pleaded innocent. Federal district court judge John J. Sirica then issued a gag order banning all witnesses and potential witnesses from talking to the press in order to ensure a fair trial, which did not commence until January 8, 1973. The gag order served to minimize media publicity over the event. Most newspapers endorsed Nixon in the election, in which he won all but one state and 60 percent of the popular vote.

Examining Cartoon 1:
"If There's an Agent 16 Listening . . ."

"IF THERE'S AN AGENT 16 LISTENING — YOUR WIFE WANTS YOU TO PICK UP A CHICKEN ON YOUR WAY HOME,,,,"

About the Cartoon

One of the first details the public learned about the June 17 break-in at the Democratic National Committee offices at the Watergate complex was that the burglars had been involved in wiretapping, or "bugging," the office. Wiretapping was by then a common law enforcement practice but was legal only for police officials with a warrant or court order. In this cartoon, Mike Peters avoids direct attacks on the practice of wiretapping or political espionage and does not accuse Nixon or his aides of wrongdoings. Rather, he takes the scenario of secret eavesdropping going on at the Democratic

Party offices and makes a joke of the situation by having an office worker pass a message on to whomever might be listening. Her knowledge of being listened to and the banal nature of her message suggests that such bugging is a silly endeavor that may not be very "secret" after all. The drawing is an example of what have been called "gag cartoons"—cartoons that focus more on humor for its own sake rather than direct political attacks.

About the Cartoonist

Mike Peters's cartooning career began in 1966 after he was drafted by the U.S. Army and started drawing cartoons for a military base newspaper at Fort Leonard Wood in Missouri. He has been the political cartoonist for the *Dayton Daily News* since 1969 and won a Pulitzer Prize for editorial cartooning in 1981. His cartoons have been collected in several books, including *The Nixon Chronicles*.

Examining Cartoon 2:

"Strange—They All Seem to Have Some Connection . . ."

"STRANGE—THEY ALL SEEM TO HAVE SOME
CONNECTION WITH THIS PLACE"

About the Cartoon

Washington Post cartoonist Herbert Block was a frequent critic of Richard Nixon, both before and after the Watergate scandal broke. This was one of the first of many Watergate cartoons Block drew following news of the arrest of five men at the Watergate office complex on June 17, 1972 (it was first published on June 23). Block attempts to link the scandal with other Nixon controversies that had been the subject of prior cartoons. The "Bugging Case" refers to the June 17, 1972, break-in itself; the men caught in the Democratic National Committee offices had wiretapping, or "bugging," devices in their possession. The "Nixon Fund Scandals" refers to allegations that the president and his campaign organization had broken laws in soliciting political contributions from corporations and individuals; it was later revealed that Nixon's reelection organization did in fact collect millions of dollars in illegal donations. "Intervention in I.T.T. Case" refers to a government settlement of an antitrust suit against the International Telephone and Telegraph Corporation. Critics, including Block, believed that the decision to settle rather than prosecute the case had been influenced by the company's pledge to help finance the 1972 Republican National Convention. Block suggests in this cartoon that the Watergate break-in is one of many improprieties that prove the Nixon administration is corrupt.

About the Cartoonist

Herbert Block, better known by his pseudonym "Herblock," was a multi-award winning editorial cartoonist who worked for the *Washington Post* newspaper from 1945 until his death in 2001. Prior to that he drew cartoons for the *Chicago Daily News* and the Newspaper Enterprise Association (NEA), as well as for the U.S. Army during World War II. Most of his work focuses on national and international events and issues. Richard Nixon had been a frequent target of Block's cartoons since the 1950s, when Nixon was vice president under Dwight D. Eisenhower.

From *Herblock Special Report* (New York: W.W. Norton, 1974). Reprinted with permission.

Chapter 2

The Scandal Deepens

Preface

At the beginning of 1973 Watergate was still a relatively minor story. In January the trial of the five arrested burglars (James McCord, Frank Sturgis, Virgilio Gonzalez, Bernard L. Barker, and Eugenio Martinez) and two other Nixon campaign officials (E. Howard Hunt and G. Gordon Liddy) began under Judge John Sirica. In the middle of the trial, Hunt, Sturgis, Gonzalez, Barker, and Martinez changed their pleas from innocent to guilty. McCord and Liddy did not change their pleas and were convicted of conspiracy, burglary, and illegal wiretapping. The federal prosecutors argued that Liddy, who had been general counsel to the Committee to Re-elect the President (CRP), had instigated the Watergate break-in without informing or getting authorization from his superiors. Sirica declared on February 2 that he was "not satisfied" that the full story was being disclosed, but had no evidence to back up his suspicions that other Nixon administration officials might be involved. He sentenced all the defendants to long terms, but held out the possibility of reducing them if the convicted burglars cooperated with continuing investigations on who authorized the break-in.

Within the next few months, several events combined to make Watergate a far larger story. Sirica's offer bore fruit when McCord, one of the convicted burglars, admitted in a letter to the judge that he and the other defendants had been under pressure to plead guilty and not tell all they knew about the case, that perjury had been committed at the trial, and that others, notably former attorney general and CRP head John Mitchell, knew of the break-in. As criminal investigators followed up on McCord's claims, soon other CRP and White House officials began to talk before government prosecutors. On April 30, President Nixon dismissed several of his top aides and announced that the Department of Justice would appoint a special prosecutor to handle all Watergate cases and investigations.

On May 18, 1973, Archibald Cox was named special prosecutor for Watergate. The previous day a special Senate committee began televised hearings on Watergate. Former White House counsel John Dean testified in June that White House officials, including Nixon himself, had engaged in an organized effort to hinder the criminal investigation of the Watergate break-in and to destroy evidence linking it to the Nixon administration. In addition, Dean stated, the Nixon administration had engaged in other questionable activities, including using the Internal Revenue Service and other government agencies to harass political opponents.

Nixon denied most of Dean's charges, and the case seemed to rest on whom the American public should believe. Then in July, the Senate committee discovered the existence of a White House taping system that had recorded most of the president's workplace conversations the previous two years. This seemed to provide a way of testing the truthfulness of what was being said and reported about Watergate. Both the Senate and the special prosecutor's office requested that Nixon turn over tapes for their inspection. Nixon refused to comply, arguing that as president he needed to protect the privacy and confidentiality of his conversations. The tape dispute came to a crisis on October 20, when Nixon told his attorney general to fire Cox; the attorney general instead resigned, and Nixon went on to dismiss Cox. Public outcry over this incident, which became known as the "Saturday Night Massacre," compelled Nixon to surrender the tapes in question and to appoint a new independent special prosecutor for Watergate. By the end of 1973, growing numbers of Americans were discussing the possibility of impeaching the president and removing him from office, and it seemed increasingly unlikely that Nixon would serve out his full second term.

Examining Cartoon 1:
The President's Defense

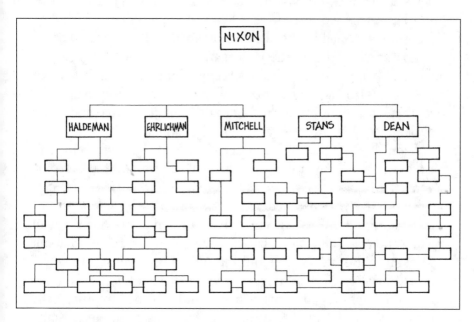

About the Cartoon

Editorial cartoons can take many forms, not all of which use caricatures. This simple drawing, first published in the *Philadelphia Inquirer* on May 23, 1973, shows an organizational chart listing President Richard Nixon's key aides, all of whom were being implicated to some extent in the Watergate affair by press and congressional investigations. But the line between these aides and the president himself is conspicuous by its absence. The drawing is a visual representation of the president's repeated assertion that he personally knew nothing about the Watergate break-in and cover-up. The cartoon suggests that these claims are questionable; it is unlikely that the president had no connection to a scandal that had tarred his closest advisers. H.R. Haldeman was Nixon's chief of staff. John Ehrlichman was Nixon's assistant for domestic affairs. Both resigned their posts on April 30, 1973. John Mitchell was attorney general before resigning in 1972 to head Nixon's reelection campaign organization, the Committee for the Reelection of the President (CRP or CREEP). Maurice Stans was the finance chairman of CRP, which was at the center of many activities that comprised the Watergate scandal. John Dean was counsel to the president until his dismissal on April 30, 1973. All the people named in the cartoon except Stans and Nixon himself eventually served time in prison for Watergate-related crimes.

About the Cartoonist
Tony Auth was a medical illustrator who began to draw political cartoons in response to the Vietnam War. He joined the staff of the *Philadelphia Inquirer* in 1971. He has won several awards, including a Pulitzer Prize and an Overseas Press Club Award. He also illustrates children's books.

Examining Cartoon 2:
"Guilty, Guilty, Guilty!!"

About the Cartoon

In 1975 Garry Trudeau became the first comic strip artist to win a Pulitzer Prize for editorial cartooning (the award traditionally went to the creators of single panel political cartoons). His *Doonesbury* comic strip, which features depictions of both real people and fictional characters, is sometimes placed in the editorial pages of the newspaper rather than the comic strip section. Newspapers have sometimes chosen to drop the strip because they deemed it too controversial. Dozens of newspapers refused to run the May 29, 1973, installment of *Doonesbury* reprinted here. The cartoon features recurring character Mark Slackmeyer, a campus radio show announcer. Slackmeyer eagerly expresses his opinion of former attorney general John Mitchell, then under suspicion for his role in the Watergate break-in and subsequent cover-up. The *Washington Post* editorialized that "if anyone is going to find any defendant guilty, it's going to be the due process of justice, not a comic strip artist. We cannot have one standard for the news pages and another for the comics." Mitchell was eventually indicted in 1974 and found guilty in 1975 of conspiracy, obstruction of justice, and perjury.

About the Cartoonist

Garry Trudeau began his cartooning career while attending Yale University; his *Doonesbury* comic strip evolved from the *Bull Tales* strip for the student newspaper. *Doonesbury*, nationally syndicated since 1970, appears in hundreds of newspapers. Trudeau has also written and produced plays and television programs.

Examining Cartoon 3:
"I Want YOUR Tapes . . ."

About the Cartoon

This cartoon is a takeoff on the famous World War I recruiting poster in which a pointing Uncle Sam declares, "I want YOU for the U.S. Army." It combines two important Watergate elements—Senator Sam Ervin (dressed as Uncle Sam) and the Nixon tapes. Ervin, a Democratic senator from North Carolina, gained national fame when he chaired the Senate Select Committee to Investigate Campaign Practices. Also known as the "Watergate Committee," it was established in February 1973 and began televised public hearings in May. The folksy Ervin became a national figure as many Americans watched him question Nixon administration officials. In July the committee discovered the existence of a White House taping system that had apparently been secretly recording most of Nixon's conversations in the White House. The committee issued a subpoena for the tapes. Nixon refused to release the tapes, leading to a legal standoff that lasted for months. The cartoon first appeared in the *San Franscisco Chronicle* on July 27, 1973, shortly after Ervin had called for the White House to release the tapes.

About the Cartoonist

Robert Graysmith worked for the *San Francisco Chronicle* as an illustrator and political cartoonist from 1968 to 1983. He has also written and illustrated several nonfiction crime books including *Zodiac* and *The Murder of Bob Crane.*

Examining Cartoon 4:

"Why, It's Law-and-Order-Man"

About the Cartoon

Throughout his first term Richard Nixon portrayed himself as a president devoted to bringing "law and order" to a country riven with divisions and dissent. However, when the Watergate scandal broke Nixon repeatedly evoked "executive privilege" in refusing to hand over tapes or otherwise cooperate with congressional and judicial inquiries into possible illegalities of his administration. Nixon argued that executive privilege is rooted in the constitutional separation of powers between the executive, legislative, and judicial branches. He also maintained that the president needs to protect the privacy of discussions with top aides in order to function effectively. However, Doug Marlette suggests in this 1973 cartoon that Nixon was attempting to use the principle to cover up unsavory or illegal deeds he and his staff may have done—an ironic turn of events for the supposedly "law and order" president.

About the Cartoonist

Doug Marlette was the cartoonist for the *Charlotte Observer* from 1972 to 1987, and the *Atlanta Constitution* from 1987 to 1989, where he won a Pulitzer Prize. He is also the creator of the comic strip *Kudzu.*

Examining Cartoon 5:
"I Cannot Tell a Lie"

The Boston Globe

HAVE I MADE PERFECTLY CLEAR . . . THAT I CANNOT TELL A LIE.

About the Cartoon
On August 15, 1973, after most of the newsworthy witnesses at the Senate Watergate hearings had testified, Nixon made a nationally televised address in which he again asserted his innocence concerning the Watergate break-in and resulting cover-up. He urged the

American people to put their "backward-looking obsession with Watergate" behind them. The speech was similar to ones he had made before and would make again. The president's assertions of innocence were contradicted by some of the witnesses the public saw testify in the televised Senate hearings, raising the issue of Nixon's truthfulness.

In this cartoon, first published in the *Boston Globe* the day after Nixon's speech, Paul Szep comments on Nixon's honesty by comparing him with America's first president, George Washington. The work is a reference to (and parody of) the famous tale from Mason Weems's ninteenth-century biography of Washington. Weems tells of how Washington as a child cut down his father's cherry tree, then confesses his misdeed by stating, "I cannot tell a lie." That story, which in all likelihood never really happened, is part of American lore and of Washington's historic image as an utterly honest and trustworthy person. By drawing Nixon in Washington's clothes and wig in a way that looks humorously inappropriate, and by prefacing Washington's statement with a phrase Nixon used often, Szep suggests that the notion that Nixon is as honest as Washington is just as ludicrous.

About the Cartoonist

Paul Szep, a native of Canada, worked in advertising and fashion illustration before being hired as the editorial cartoonist of the *Boston Globe* in 1966. He has won two Pulitzer Prizes.

Examining Cartoon 6:
"I'd Like to Appoint One of You Attorney General . . ."

"I'd like to appoint one of you Attorney General and the other Special Prosecutor."

About the Cartoon

An important turning point in the Watergate scandal occurred when President Richard Nixon attempted to fire Archibald Cox, the special prosecutor in charge of the investigation. Cox, a Harvard Law School professor, was selected on May 18, 1973, by newly appointed attorney general Elliot Richardson to be special prosecutor and take over for the federal prosecutors who had been investigating the affair. When Cox learned in July that Nixon had made tapes of most of his conversations as president, he sued Nixon to obtain some of them and refused Nixon's counteroffer of edited written summaries. On October 20, 1973, Nixon ordered Richardson to fire Cox, but Richardson instead resigned. Nixon finally succeeded in dismissing Cox. Nixon's public approval ratings tumbled, however, and a few days later he agreed to turn over the tapes subpoenaed by Cox and to appoint a new special prosecutor, Leon Jaworski.

By this time the Watergate scandal had attracted considerable international as well as national attention. This October 21, 1973, cartoon by English cartoonist Keith Waite shows Richard Nixon finding only one person he could trust in filling the shoes of Richardson and Cox—himself. Unfortunately for Nixon, this option was not available in real life.

About the Cartoonist

Keith Waite drew editorial cartoons for the English newspapers the *Sun* and the *Mirror*.

Examining Cartoon 7:
"Piranha"

About the Cartoon

According to many Nixon defenders, a major, if not the sole, cause of his Watergate problems was biased media coverage. This cartoon by Karl Hubenthal portrays Nixon as a helpless victim of vicious and biased attacks by such media organizations as the *New York Times* and the *Washington Post*. Hubenthal also criticizes special prosecutor Leon Jaworski and the federal grand jury hearing the Watergate case for leaking private testimony to the press. Hubenthal's opinion of the media is a fair representation of Nixon's own views.

About the Cartoonist

Karl Hubenthal was hired as a sports cartoonist for the *Los Angeles Examiner* in 1949 and became chief editorial cartoonist for that newspaper in 1955. He was one of President Nixon's staunchest defenders in the editorial cartooning profession. He retired in 1980 after winning numerous awards.

Chapter 3

Fall of a President

Preface

On February 6, 1974, the House of Representatives voted to start impeachment proceedings against President Nixon. (The Constitution gives Congress the power to impeach and remove the president and other government officials for "treason, bribery, and other high crimes and misdemeanors.") It directed the House Judiciary Committee, chaired by Peter Rodino, to begin an investigation on whether grounds existed to remove the president.

Nixon's impeachment seemed more likely on March 1, 1974, after a federal grand jury indicted seven ranking Nixon aides, including John Ehrlichman, H.R. Haldeman, and John Mitchell, for various Watergate-related crimes. The jury, after hearing evidence presented by Leon Jaworski, a Texas attorney who had replaced Archibald Cox as Watergate special prosecutor, chose to name Nixon himself as an "unindicted coconspirator." Both Jaworski and the House Judiciary Committee issued subpoenas to produce White House tapes Nixon had refused to provide on request (although Nixon had agreed in late 1973 to relinquish nine tapes that had been subpoenaed by Cox, he refused to release any more). Jaworski wanted the tapes to help build his case for the prosecution in the upcoming trials of the defendants indicted on March 1. The House Judiciary Committee wanted the tapes for its own investigation of the president. Nixon tried to satisfy their request on April 30 by releasing hundreds of pages of transcripts of White House tapes, but Congress and Jaworski continued to press for the tapes themselves. The transcripts, which revealed that Nixon often used ethnic slurs and obscenities, proved damaging to Nixon's public image.

Nixon continued to ignore subpoenas for the tapes until the Supreme Court ruled 8-0 that he must turn them over. Some of the tapes he finally surrendered revealed that the president had known about the Watergate incident and had tried to hinder its investigation from the beginning; this revelation caused him to lose most of his remaining public support. The House Judiciary Committee approved three articles of impeachment. The articles accused Nixon of obstruction of justice in the Watergate scandal, abuse of presidential powers, and attempting to impede the impeachment process by refusing the tape subpoenas. The next step was to be a vote by the full House, followed by a Senate trial. After some vacillation, Nixon resigned his office on August 9, 1974, avoiding impeachment.

Nixon was succeeded by Gerald Ford, a former member of Congress who was appointed by Nixon himself to be vice president following the resignation of Spiro T. Agnew because of an unrelated scandal. On September 8, 1974, Ford issued a presidential pardon for Nixon. The other Watergate defendants were not pardoned. In a trial lasting from October 1974 to January 1975, Ehrlichman, Haldeman, and Mitchell were each convicted of conspiracy, obstruction of justice, and perjury and were sentenced to prison terms.

Examining Cartoon 1:
"Do I Smell Blood?"

"Do I smell blood?"

About the Cartoon

On February 6, 1974, the House of Representatives voted to start impeachment proceedings against President Nixon. Under the U.S. Constitution, the House has the power to impeach or formally charge the president or other government officials. Impeached officials are tried before the Senate and removed from office if found guilty. The House Judiciary Committee ultimately approved three articles of impeachment against Nixon, who resigned before the matter came up before the full House or the Senate.

Impeachment was a constitutional device that had been only used once before against a president in U.S. history. Many people believed it would be a destabilizing force at a bad time when the U.S. was faced with foreign policy challenges. Among these challenges was dealing with the Soviet Union, a Communist superpower and America's cold war rival. Cartoonist Tom Curtis illustrates possible international repercussions of impeaching a U.S. president. His shark, decorated with the hammer and sickle, symbols of communism, represents the Soviet Union eager to take advantage of political turmoil in the United States caused by calls for impeachment.

About the Cartoonist
Tom Curtis was staff editorial cartoonist of the *Milwaukee Sentinel* during the time Richard Nixon was president. He was recognized as one of the nation's leading politically conservative cartoonists.

Examining Cartoon 2:
"He's Chewing Up the Congress!"

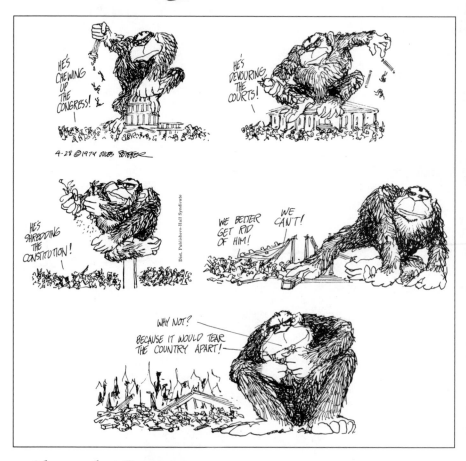

About the Cartoon

The cartoons of Jules Feiffer combine the multipanel structure of comic strips with the social and political commentary of editorial cartoons. In this example, which first appeared in the *Village Voice* on April 28, 1974, he questions the view that impeaching President Nixon would be divisive to the country, suggesting that Nixon himself is the menace to the country by defying congressional and judicial proceedings and exceeding his constitutional powers as president.

About the Cartoonist

Jules Feiffer has a large body of work including plays, motion picture screenplays, and novels. He began drawing *Feiffer,* a weekly cartoon, for the *Village Voice* in 1956. He won a Pulitzer Prize for editorial cartooning in 1986.

Examining Cartoon 3:
"I Didn't Know It Was Loaded!"

"I DIDN'T KNOW IT WAS LOADED!"

About the Cartoon

On July 24, 1974, the Supreme Court unanimously ruled that Nixon must give to the presiding judge in the Watergate trials taped conversations he had been withholding. These tapes, transcripts of which were made available to the general public on August 5, became known as the "smoking gun" (smoke being evidence that a gun had been fired). They included conversations made on June 23, 1972, six days after the Watergate break-in, in which Nixon told his aides to use the CIA to tell the FBI to back off certain avenues in investigating the Watergate incident. The "smoking gun" proved that Nixon was personally involved in the Watergate cover-up, contrary to his previous public assurance that he did not even know about the cover-up until months later. Nixon, in a statement made when the tapes were made public, said, "I did not realize the extent of the implications, which these conversations might now appear to have." In addition, he admitted that his May 22, 1973, statement that he acted solely out of national security concerns was not fully truthful. Cartoonist Pat Oliphant responded to the stunning revelation with this depiction of Nixon in gangster's clothing holding a smoking gun. The implication is that Nixon's credibility in professing surprise at the incriminating information on the tapes is just as questionable as a gangster's professing surprise that his gun was in fact loaded.

A trademark of Oliphant cartoons is the inclusion of Punk, a penguin who makes his own asides and comments on the cartoon. In this instance, Punk questions Vice President Gerald Ford, soon to become president, on whether he accepts Nixon's veracity. Ford, who had received personal assurances of innocence from Nixon when he agreed to become vice president, later pardoned Nixon for any crimes he may have committed.

About the Cartoonist

Patrick Oliphant is a native of Australia who moved to the United States in 1964 to become editorial cartoonist for the *Denver Post*. He moved to the *Washington Star* in 1975, then became an independent syndicated cartoonist; his work appears in five hundred newspapers in the United States and other countries. He has won several awards, including a 1967 Pulitzer Prize.

Examining Cartoon 4:
"The King Is Dead . . ."

THE KING IS DEAD . . . LONG LIVE THE PRESIDENCY!

About the Cartoon
President Richard Nixon, facing almost certain impeachment by Congress, announced his resignation on August 8, 1974, effective at noon on August 9. The August 9 edition of the *Los Angeles Times* featured this cartoon by staff cartoonist Paul Conrad. It shows the fallen crown of a deposed king. The crown is decorated with tape reels that refer to Nixon's infamous tapes and dollar signs signifying

the financial scandals that dogged Nixon and his campaign organization.

Many critics had argued that Nixon often acted more like a monarch than a president of a republic. This was especially true during Watergate, when some thought his conduct suggested that he considered the president to be above the law and beyond the control of Congress and the courts. Conrad, like other cartoonists, had frequently depicted Nixon as a king. In a previous cartoon, Conrad drew a crowned and robed Nixon quoting from William Shakespeare's play *Richard II* ("O that I were as great as my grief, or lesser than my name! Or that I could forget what I have been! Or not remember what I must be now!") In this cartoon, Nixon's resignation is seen by Conrad not as a blow to the U.S. presidency, but as a vindication of the American ideal of an elected and accountable leader—an ideal that has been threatened by Nixon's actions.

About the Cartoonist

Paul Conrad was editorial cartoonist for the *Los Angeles Times* from 1964 until his retirement in 1993; he continues to draw cartoons for the Los Angeles Times Syndicate. He is a three-time recipient of the Pulitzer Prize for editorial cartooning. Conrad was the only political cartoonist on President Richard Nixon's "Enemies List"—a compilation of media and political figures cataloged by Nixon and his staff that was publicly revealed in Senate Watergate hearings in 1973.

Examining Cartoon 5:
"You've Got to Admit We're Getting Watergate Behind Us"

"You've got to admit we're getting Watergate behind us."

About the Cartoon

Vice President Gerald Ford assumed the office of president on August 9, 1974, following Richard Nixon's resignation. Ford was a longtime member of Congress with a sterling reputation for honesty and no real connection to the Watergate scandal. His first words to the American people as president were, "Your long national nightmare is over." Despite his assurances, Watergate continued to persist as a national issue, as this cartoon by Draper Hill suggests. Ford is shown wrestling a snake whose features resemble those of Richard Nixon. The writing on the snake refers to controversial events related to Nixon and to the Watergate scandal, including the criminal trial of Nixon aides that ended in January 1975, expenses related to the transition, including Nixon's move to San Clemente, California, and the question of what control Nixon should maintain over his unreleased tapes. But undoubtedly the most notorious event in the eyes of many was Ford's announcement on September 8, 1974, that he had issued a presidential pardon "for all offenses against the United States which . . . Nixon has committed, or may have committed" during his presidency. Public reaction against the pardon was strong, with many people believing (without proof) that Ford and Nixon had made some sort of deal in which Nixon agreed to resign in exchange for being pardoned. Public disapproval of Nixon's pardon likely contributed to Ford's defeat in the 1976 presidential election.

About the Cartoonist

Draper Hill has been the editorial cartoonist for several newspapers, including the *Commercial Appeal* (Memphis) from 1971 to 1976, and the *Detroit News* from 1976 to 1999. He has written several books on the history of political cartoons.

Examining Cartoon 6:
"Cancel My Appointments . . ."

"CANCEL MY APPOINTMENTS ,,,,, THIS ONE MAY TAKE AWHILE."

About the Cartoon

By the time Richard Nixon passed away in April 1994, the Watergate scandal was two decades old. Nixon remained a source of division even in passing. Some of the people who eulogized him, including President Bill Clinton, argued that Watergate was only part of Nixon's legacy, which also included many years of public service and numerous accomplishments as president. Others maintained that the Watergate disgrace was his primary legacy. Cartoonist Jim Borgman captures some of the ambiguous public feeling on Nixon twenty years after Watergate in this cartoon of Nixon approaching the "pearly gates" of heaven with his characteristic "victory" pose, leaving St. Peter to sort out and judge what had been a long and complex life.

About the Cartoonist

Jim Borgman was a college art major when Nixon resigned in 1974. Since 1976 he has been the editorial cartoonist for the *Cincinnati Enquirer*. Borgman won a Pulitzer Prize in 1991. He is also the coauthor of the comic strip *Zits*.

Chronology

June 17, 1972
Five men are caught breaking in to the offices of the Democratic National Committee at the Watergate apartment and office complex. One is James W. McCord, security director for the Committee to Reelect the President (CRP).

June 23, 1972
Nixon approves a plan to interfere with the FBI investigation on Watergate; the conversation is secretly taped by the president.

September 15, 1972
The five Watergate burglars and two others, G. Gordon Liddy and E. Howard Hunt, are indicted in a federal district court.

November 7, 1972
Nixon is reelected president by a huge margin.

January 8, 1973
The trial of the Watergate burglars begins. Five of the defendants change their pleas from innocent to guilty during the trial. McCord and Liddy are convicted on January 30.

February 7, 1973
The Senate votes to establish a Select Committee on Presidential Campaign Activities. The committee, also known as the Watergate Committee, is chaired by Sam Ervin, a Democrat from North Carolina.

March 21, 1973
White House counsel John Dean tells Nixon that there is a "cancer" growing on the presidency.

March 23, 1973
A letter by James McCord to Judge Sirica is read by Sirica in open court; McCord charges that defendants had pleaded guilty under pressure and that perjury was committed at the trial.

April 6, 1973
Dean begins negotiations for cooperating with federal Watergate prosecutors.

April 17, 1973
Presidential press secretary Ronald L. Ziegler says that all previous White House statements on Watergate are "inoperative."

April 30, 1973
President Richard Nixon announces the dismissal of John Dean and the resignations of top aides H.R. Haldeman and John Ehrlichman. Attorney General Richard Kleindienst also resigns and is replaced by Elliot Richardson.

May 18, 1973
Richardson appoints Archibald Cox to be special prosecutor for the Watergate case.

May–October 1973
The Senate Watergate Committee holds public televised hearings.

June 25, 1973
Dean testifies before the Watergate Committee; he describes a political espionage program conducted by the White House and asserts that Nixon was involved in the cover-up of the Watergate break-in.

July 16, 1973
White House aide Alexander Butterfield, testifying before the Senate Watergate Committee, reveals the existence of a White House taping system.

July 25, 1973
Nixon refuses to release White House tapes to Cox, arguing that such a concession would jeopardize the "independence of the three branches of government."

October 10, 1973
Vice President Spiro Agnew resigns in the face of tax evasion and other charges unrelated to the Watergate scandal.

October 12, 1973
Nixon nominates Gerald R. Ford to replace Agnew as vice president.

October 20, 1973
The "Saturday Night Massacre" occurs; Nixon orders Attorney General Richardson to fire Cox. Richardson refuses and resigns. The deputy attorney general is dismissed after refusing to fire Cox. Finally, Solicitor General Robert Bork dismisses the special prosecutor.

October 23, 1973
Nixon agrees to release the tapes Cox had sought.

October 30, 1973
The House Judiciary Committee starts consideration of possible impeachment procedures.

November 1, 1973
Nixon appoints Leon Jaworski to be the new Watergate special prosecutor.

November 21, 1973
The public learns that one of the tapes Cox wanted has a mysterious $18\frac{1}{2}$ minute gap in it.

February 6, 1974
The House votes to proceed with a Nixon impeachment inquiry and gives the House Judiciary Committee broad subpoena powers.

February 25, 1974
In a nationally televised speech, Nixon vows never to resign from office.

March 1, 1974
A federal grand jury indicts Haldeman, Ehrlichman, John Mitchell, Gordon Strachan, Robert Mardian, Kenneth Parkinson, and Charles Colson for covering up the Watergate burglary; Nixon is named as an unindicted coconspirator.

April 30, 1974
Nixon releases more edited transcripts of tapes, which are noteworthy for their frankness and for adding the phrase "expletive deleted" to the nation's vocabulary.

May 7, 1974
Nixon's lawyer, James D. St. Clair, announces that no more White House tapes will be turned over to the special prosecutor or the House Judiciary Committee.

May 9, 1974
The House Judiciary Committee begins impeachment hearings.

July 24, 1974
The U.S. Supreme Court rules 8-0 in *United States v. Nixon* that the president must turn over the White House tapes requested by Jaworski.

July 27–30, 1974
The House Judiciary Committee votes to recommend three articles of impeachment against Nixon.

August 5, 1974
The "smoking gun" tape from June 23, 1972, is released to the public; it reveals that Nixon was part of the Watergate cover-up early on.

August 8, 1974
Nixon announces his resignation from office, effective noon the next day.

August 9, 1974
Gerald Ford becomes the nation's thirty-eighth president.

September 8, 1974
President Ford gives Nixon a "full, free, and absolute pardon" for whatever crimes the former president may have committed.

For Further Research

Books on Watergate

Carl Bernstein and Bob Woodward, *All the President's Men.* New York: Simon and Schuster, 1974.

Daniel Cohen, *Watergate: Deception in the White House.* Brookfield, CT: Millbrook, 1998.

Len Colodny and Robert Gettlin, *Silent Coup: The Removal of Richard Nixon.* New York: St. Martin's Press, 1990.

Elizabeth Drew, *Washington Journal: The Events of 1973–1974.* New York: Random House, 1975.

Mark E. Dudley, *United States v. Nixon (1974): Presidential Powers.* New York: Twenty-First Century Books, 1994.

Fred Emery, *Watergate: The Corruption of American Politics and the Fall of Richard Nixon.* New York: Times Books, 1994.

Barbara Silberdick Feinberg, *Watergate: Scandal in the White House.* New York: Watts, 1990.

David K. Fremon, *The Watergate Scandal in American History.* Springfield, NJ: Enslow, 1998.

Michael A. Genovese, *The Watergate Crisis.* Westport, CT: Greenwood, 1999.

Jeff Hay, ed., *Richard M. Nixon: Presidents and Their Decisions.* San Diego: Greenhaven, 2001.

Stanley I. Kutler, *The Wars of Watergate: The Last Crisis of Richard Nixon.* New York: Knopf, 1990.

Stanley I. Kutler, ed., *Abuse of Power: The New Nixon Tapes*. New York: Touchstone Books, 1998.

Victor Lasky, *It Didn't Start with Watergate*. New York: Dial, 1977.

J. Anthony Lukas, *Nightmare: The Underside of the Nixon Years*. New York: Penguin, 1988.

Kim McQuaid, *The Anxious Years: America in the Vietnam-Watergate Era*. New York: BasicBooks, 1989.

Richard Nixon, *RN: The Memoirs of Richard Nixon*. New York: Grosset and Dunlap, 1978.

Myron J. Smith, *Watergate: An Annotated Bibliography of Sources in English, 1972–1982*. Metuchen, NJ: Scarecrow, 1983.

Political Cartoon Books

Amon Carter Museum of Western Art, *The Image of America in Caricature and Cartoon*. Fort Worth, TX: Amon Carter Museum of Western Art, 1976.

Tony Auth, *Behind the Lines*. Boston: Houghton Mifflin, 1977.

Herbert Block, *Herblock Special Report*. New York: Norton, 1974.

Paul Conrad, *The King and Us*. Los Angeles: Clymer, 1974.

Jules Feiffer, *Feiffer on Nixon: The Cartoon Presidency*. New York: Random House, 1974.

Roger A. Fischer, *Them Damned Pictures: Explorations in American Political Cartoon Art*. North Haven, CT: Archon, 1996.

Ranan R. Lurie, *Nixon-Rated Cartoons*. New York: Quadrangle, 1974.

Mike Peters, *The Nixon Chronicles*. Dayton, OH: Lorenz, 1976.

Paul P. Somers Jr., *Editorial Cartooning and Caricature: A Reference Guide*. Westport, CT: Greenwood, 1998.

G.B. Trudeau, *Guilty, Guilty, Guilty! A Doonesbury Book*. New York: Holt, Rinehart, and Winston, 1974.

Web Resources

Caroline and Erwin Swann Collection of Caricature and Cartoon
http://lcweb.loc.gov/rr/print/coll/230_swan.html#Relatedout

The website is assocated with a collection of caricatures and cartoons that was donated to the Library of Congress in 1977. It includes a searchable catalog of cartoon images and a listing of other library and online cartoon collections.

Illusion and Delusion: The Watergate Decade

www.journale.com/watergate

This is an online photograph essay of the Watergate era that includes portraits of key players in the scandal.

Nixon Tapes

www.nara.gov/nixon/tapes/index.html

In this website, the National Archives and Records Adminstration (NARA) provides public access to 1,284 hours of the tapes President Nixon recorded.

Watergate

http://vcepolitics.com/watergate

Constructed by an Australian political science teacher, this website provides a chronological overview of Watergate and links to speeches and other primary sources.

Watergate 25th Aniversary

www.cnn.com/ALLPOLITICS/1997/gen/resources/watergate/sites.
html

This website, a coproduction of Cable News Network (CNN) and *Time* magazine, contains numerous links to articles, photographs, timelines, political cartoons, presidential transcripts, and other Watergate websites.

Index